The Distance Between

poems
by
Julie Valin

Top Shelf Poetry Series #1

Six Ft. Swells Press

After Hours Poetry

The Distance Between
Copyright 2011 © Julie Valin
2nd edition, June 2012

ISBN 978-0985307516

Six Ft. Swells Press
Top Shelf Poetry Series #1
Grass Valley, CA 95945
sixfootswells@yahoo.com
www.AfterHoursPoetry.com

Editor & Publisher: Todd Cirillo
Cover photos: Matt Amott, Betsy Fasbinder
Cover & Book Design: Julie Valin, *The Word Boutique*

Acknowledgments:
New Heaven, Curse Me – Chiron Review (2011)
a version of *The Final Score* – Primal Urge (Aug/Sept. 2011)
A Poet's Life – Red Fez (May 2011)
Heavy Metal Summer; Bad Music Hostage –
Savage Melodies & Last Call Serenades (Six Ft. Swells Press 2010)
Kicking a Bull in the Balls – Heavy Bear (2009)
Bukowski Writes My Best Poem – Night Songs for Heavy
Dreamers (Six Ft. Swells Press 2006)

Get in the Car:
Cannibal Drake, my fave poetry editor and comrade
extraordinaire; The "other" Todd who is the best prompter
and listener I ever met; Heather D. with her perpetual
awesomeness and love of funnel cakes; Annie and her
matching poetic heart. Let's burn rubber and let our hair fly.

Punk Rock Baby Mama

Julie Valin was born to fall in love. She has been falling in love all her life: from her youngest memories of the moon to her teenage heavy metal make-out sessions, to college all-nighters, marriage and motherhood. Her poems in *The Distance Between* capture life's moments clearly like pictures in a frame—showing how a woman progresses from late night punk rock shows and scandals to responsible mother and partner. Yet, she continues to be that midnight rendezvous and the morning wake-up call. Eggs over-easy and hot wings. A baby in one hand and a cocktail in the other. All the while maintaining the ability to find love in all of it, even when she rips the concept open to expose it for what it is: a terrible gamble that eventually pays off. That is what I love about Julie.

There are moments in this book that make us feel like perverted voyeurs in the night peeping into someone else's miseries and triumphs. Some moments we want to scream "don't believe him!" Others make us want to join the party, be her rebound lover, offer to babysit her child so she can go out on a Friday evening, laugh at that first kiss and comfort her when the last one has blown away.

Anyone with a true heart will recognize these poems. They are clear, clean and gorgeous in their simplicity. This is where Julie truly shines and shows us that she is one of the top American poets of this generation.

I say, go ahead and take a peek, the moon will light your way, and Julie will show you what love is.

--Todd Cirillo, poet, editor
1:16 a.m. 8/5/11

Between the Covers

To the girl I was
who still comes around
when the kid is asleep and the moon is calling—
and to the man who loves us both.

-o-

....

Dismissal

Hello blank page
you thought you'd sneak by me
but I found you
and it's time for you to go.

....

A Poet's Life

It doesn't have to be
like his—
all whiskey
and loneliness,
crumbled papers
piled around
a manual typewriter
at 3 a.m.
and beautiful women
showing up at all hours.

It can be this simple:
oatmeal for breakfast,
a 9 to 5 job,
a peaceful walk
with the dog
at dusk,
Coltrane on the stereo,
red wine with mac and cheese,
and a quiet bliss
as I watch my husband
through the window
mow the lawn.
Night after night
my lamp left on
while he sleeps
so I can read
in bed,
our arms
tangled
in dreams.

....

Silence, That Dreadful Bell

Even pure silence
creates a hum
that booms
in my ears.
There are long days
that are too wide
and detailed
to love any-
thing, or
answer one
pressing question.
I go on, fill my head
with the blues,
have a beer
in the park
out of a paper bag
at 2:00 p.m.
without you.
Only to walk
around the edges
of the night,
tiptoe on the carpet,
never scrape the dishes
in the sink,
hum wishes
to ourselves,
whisper
goodnight,
  so tomorrow
  sings in our sleep
  like a bell.

....

Heavy Metal Summer

My 15-year-old summer
was all sweat and musk,
sweet lust and revelation,
smeared lip smacker
and hand lotion
in the heat of his
teenage room.

It's hard to make-out
to Ozzy's Crazy Train
with all that laughing
and bass thumping,
but, we did it.
All the way
through
the first side.
When he got up
to flip the record,
it amped up my anticipation
of where we would be
carried away next,
the rise of the guitar's moan
and beating drums—
the accompaniment
to my wild exploration
of his hot love,
the room
humming with
high notes,
melodic words,
and heavy metal sunshine.

....

Walking Shadows

You're stuck

looking back
at me.

Is this how it's always going to be,

my shadow
lurching forward

to touch the tip

of yours?

....

The Final Score

She lost it
on the living room floor
with the TV blaring
and her brother
in his room at the far end
of the house.
He was a mad, bad boy,
high crew cut
like Depeche Mode, she hoped.
He was younger than her,
but rougher.
Pretty but careless,
strong but ruthless—
all the things
she wasn't
but didn't
necessarily want
to be.
There was no love,
only a surrender
of sorts
because it's always
about someone giving up
something.
Even so,
even with all that,
she didn't lose a thing,
and he walked away
smiling,
confident of his victory,
too dumb to realize
it was nothing but a draw.

....

Chagall's Painting is My Poem

- Weinstein Gallery, San Francisco

Because the painter smiles
as he dips the tip
of the brush in his palette.

Because the nude woman
on the canvas laid flat
on the floor
     and the dot of red
     at her nipple
is the same red
of the sun
burning through the window.

     Because he loves her.

Because his words are vibrant hues
and his hand is the brush moving.
Because she is the shade of flames
when he puts his convictions on paper.

Because the sun is an egg
over-easy
and there are always flowers
everywhere.

Because the painter smiles
as he dips the tip
of the brush in his palette

     and his love for her bleeds
     in all my favorite colors.

Bukowski Writes My Best Poem

I thought it honorary
to introduce
the one true poet
who taught me
simplicity
and gems
of truth.

So after reading
2 of my poems,
I chose the one of his
about green Jello
and the fat lady
on the curb
and I read it brilliantly.
The audience
ate it up.

Afterwards
the people came up
to me, loved my poem
about green Jello
and the fat lady
on the curb—

. . . *you bastard*,
even in your
absence
I can't
for the life of me

live up
to you.

....

Poetry with Intention

I hated
the well-published poet
for telling me
that my poetry
gets in the way
of my poems.

After 10 more years of writing
my heart out, moving,
marrying, mothering,
now I see the beauty
of telling it like it is.

Did it matter
when he first kissed me
that the canyon below
echoed the moonlight,
or that his lips
were firm in their intention?
What matters
is that he kissed me,
and it never stopped
being good.

··

How We Wake

Hands rise
out of heavy sheets
in a slow tingle
of limbs and skin
as they reach
their warm partners;
the constant shedding
of ourselves in sleep. . .
how we let go
like dying stars
only to take it all
back in again
when the burn of the sun
returns—

the first breath in.

Solitude

Maybe the reason you exist
for me
is so you can be
my very own island
to explore—
kind of like being alone,
together.

....

Blowing Away

I remember what he said about it—
the wind,
that time I fell in love with him
in late October.
I told him this love was
blowing me away,
and he said
that's okay, I will
hold your hand
so we can blow away together.

And then the breeze picked up,
and the leaves rustled
from where I breathed,
and he reached
for me.

....

Curse Me

*"You look like me,
and I look like no one else."*
                        -Greg Dulli

Crack my heart open, baby,
with one of your sweet,
fucked-up love songs,
the ones about sex
in the shadows
on unmade beds
in the pocket of a dirty city,
or about cocktails for two
down lover's lane
and burning up, over-the-edge
hot love with your hand down my pants
until I can't walk straight.

Curse me
with your throaty notes under my skin,
your melodic kisses, the juice
straight into the vein.

I can live famously
through your thousand
little love deaths,
each one a thousand times more
than I've ever lived once.
And when one ends—
when it's all up in flames—
I will wait for it to cool
and then play it again
and again,
yes, baby, over
and over
for you.

....

Cold Plunge

He proposed to me
in a steam bath
on my 30th birthday,
but he didn't say
the words.
I pointed that out,
and then he jumped
into the cold plunge.
But I couldn't do it,
only up to my calves.
In the hot tub
I kept looking
at the ring,
as if it was some new,
shiny scar
I will always
have with me
no matter what—
fascinating
and appalling
at the same time.

Broken

How
could you
have dropped
the world
she handed
you?

....

The Distance Between

We used to stay up
later than the moon
to talk about everything
under the sun,
and love each other
in various spontaneous locations:
the staircase,
the dining room table,
your mom's guest room
on that horrible inflatable mattress,
that chair in your room—
the upholstered one
with the wingback and high arms
that rocked and spun.

Now we have 3-minute conversations
with 2 word answers,
and what we have
isn't called sex anymore—
that word reserved only
for lustful couples—
and when we do "it"
it's only on the bed,
which we make immediately
following,
letting the wet spot
dry on its own—
the distance between us
spreading
to each corner
of the house.

....

Still Life with Sun

In all of the photographs
the sun always finds her face,
golden and bright
as if shining from within,
her eyes, universes
lit up by flashes
of future moments,
or the next burning thing
she will leave
in ashes.

If only she could
have lived in *that* moment—

when the sky captured her
in rims of fire,

his arms
reaching out from the edge
of a world that only exists
inside the frame,

to hold that radiant face
in his own hot hands,

to kiss her—

while the red sky
blazes up into itself

and the camera ignites
to catch
up to her.

Starring Us

This is the part of the movie
where I am in my room at my desk
with the chromed light spotlighting
what I'm writing, and maybe it is a split
screen with you in your room
reading your 500 page book,
and then I set my pen down,
you bookmark your page
and we both drift to the same place,
except people wouldn't want to watch this.
It would look like 2 people
staring off into space.

If they waited around long enough
maybe they would see us laugh in the car.
Or have *huevos rancheros* at the diner,
but they would have to sit
through the conversations, and if they're lucky,
the pauses in between
when the man smiles at the woman
with his knowing eyes, or reaches
around the Tabasco to touch
her hand. But they would be so bored
by that. They'd want the action. The sex.
First the robbery, and then
the wild groping in the hotel room,
their clothes flying around them
like soft, easy gunfire that feels good.

But it's not a take.

....

You and I prefer the parts that occur
when we are bigger than the screen, so big
that we are pixilated into one blur.

There's the sound of breathing.
Stan Getz is in the background.
Someone says yes.

And the audience would be left to imagine
the sun on our faces
how it hits us perfectly
as we shine together
famously.

Words on Fire

He constructed words for her
by rubbing 2 sticks together.
It took him his whole life
to formulate them
in this distinct free-flowing manner,
never to test them
on the tip of his tongue.
And then finally she stood before him,
a lonely audience,
backed by sky and stars.
And then he began to speak them,
unrehearsed,
hot in her ear
on a cool Fall evening.
His hands were his adjectives,
and his heartbeat was the verb,
his eyes were his direct modifiers
and his mouth was a metaphor
for fire-lit embers.

The word "love" he saved
for last.
She cupped it in her hands
and then she sipped it
carefully so as not to mark her tongue,
and she swallowed,
sweetness burning
all the way down.
Hot,
hot,
sweetness.

Scars

You promised
you would kiss
every one of them
if you could find them.

I would scar them
into me
all over again
if I believed you.

Pissed off at Angels

Your need to profess
your belief in angels
on Facebook
is really pissing me off.
I mean, you're the one who's Catholic,
and I don't go to church,
but even I know
that angels
aren't just a nice piece of ass.
They don't go around
giving married men advice
and sipping venti lattes,
or drive luxury SUV's
in a sea-level city,
or tell you how to find love.
A real bona fide angel
would be the woman
whose been putting up with your shit
for 22 years,
the sweet mother of your children.
The fact is,
unless you're whispering
the word in your wife's ear,
if I hear you mention angels
one more time
I'm going to kick you
in the nuts,
while all the angels
laugh their asses off
and there won't be a prayer in hell
to save you.

....

Punk Rock on the Inside

In the bathroom
with punk rock walls
of Sharpie inscriptions
like "Fuck Nicole" and
"I like boys with toys"
and "Jamie loves Matt forever"—
she walks in from the stage
to check her lipstick.
"Hi", she says,
with a bullet-red smile
and straight licorice black hair.
Swooping my bangs,
I answer a common
hello,
admiring her miniskirt
and chunky boots.

"I'm punk rock
on the inside!"
I yell to her
in my head.

She smiles again
before walking out,
the run in her stockings
trailing up the length
of her long leg,
making her nearly perfect.

I walk away from the mirror
to stand in the front row,
nodding my head
to her songs.

So Long, Cowboy Poets

You rode it hard
and got put away wet,
but I appreciate you
for your respect
of livestock,
your work ethic,
and for finding poetry
in that.

The closest
I ever come to being
a cowgirl
is I listen to Patsy Cline
on my iPod,
blasting her in my car
like she is some
Nirvana.
With the windows
all the way down,
I sing to the cars
next to me with my own twang:
   Crazy for feeling so lonely...
   and crazy
   for loving
   you....

So what if I drive
a black Toyota
with a pirate
bumper sticker—
the truth is
we can all glean poetry
from just about anything:

....

we are all roaming
the wide open range
with all its possibilities
for love
or heartache
to come
stampeding
in.

Kicking a Bull in the Balls

for Todd Cirillo

When I told him
drinking alone
is the stuff
of legends,
he said,
"I'd rather kick a bull
in the balls
than be here
alone."

With all the greats
holding up their fists
in their graves,
he got the truth
just in time—
a single barstool
in a crowded drinking hole
is not where you take
the muse by the throat.

It is the guts
it takes
to go home
to her

that will give the poems brawn
to endure.

Negotiating with Pirates

I used to glorify pirates,
their balls-out attitudes
of taking what they want,
storming the Indian seas
with their mates,
singing songs, getting rowdy,
drinking an endless supply
of booze, their eyes glinting
with all their loot

but now after seeing
the ugly truth of it all—
the raping and pillaging,
the destruction and ransoms--

I just see them as
assholes with rotten teeth.

These days
I'd settle for
2 bottles of red wine
shared equally among friends,
sailing Lake Tahoe
by the gold glow
of sunset
laughing, singing 80's songs,
and telling wild stories
of all we've conquered.

Seeking Warmth

Hail in May erases any sun that shone.
We start from scratch.
Turn the heat up, throw small logs
in the stove,
sit where it's warmest.
If even a sliver
of sun peeks
through the slats of the deck,
that is where I lay my hands.
Or we go to the window
with the rainbow beads
and face West.
But not now.
Not with all the missing sunrays
shivering behind the black clouds.
Even this blanket won't do the job,
the one you stitched a sun into
simply for this purpose.
I could run a hot bubble bath,
but that is temporary
and unreliable.

Four cities away
you might not be as cold.
You are cooking hot soup
and rubbing her feet.
You are talking about your day
and listening to hers.
There might have been a time
when you were loved even more
than you are now,
but that was more
temporary and unreliable.

....

What does it matter if it hails
in May?
There is always something warm
to cling to.
There is always another blanket
to pile on top.
It's just a matter
of seeking it out,
even in the dark places,
and being content
with what you find.

Something About the Wind

The sky had been resting
for days,
and then the wind came.
A guy at the park
asked if this is normal,
the wind,
at this time of year,
and I didn't know how to answer
because that is a funny question,
if you think about it. I mean, I don't really ever
keep track of the wind
and how much it blows
at certain times of the year,
or even last week.

So I said,
"It's, very unusual,"
because it seemed
a foreboding
and dramatic answer,
then I watched
my daughter breeze
down the slide,
her hair sticking
up with static,
and I laughed.

A candy wrapper
bounced over
to the yellow
climbing wall
and people

were running around,
chasing things.

"Windy day!"
exclaimed my daughter,
filled with excitement
for the simple truth
of things.

Getting to You

I could be barefoot
and light as smoke
on broken glass—

but why is it
that I still can't move
fast enough
to get to you?

Bad Music Hostage

I wanna know what love is.
I want you to show me... -Foreigner

Stuck at the jiffy lube,
I'm optimistic
that poetry can be found anywhere:
in the music of the cash register,
in the oily hands
of the young mechanics
who smile at the pretty girl
who dropped off her car,
in the promise of a date tonight
between the counter girl
and the manager.
"Can't stop now," she belts out, knowing
every word to all the songs
on the classic rock station, *"I've traveled so far,*
to change this lonely life," she croons
while her ponytail sways.
But after The Doobie Brothers,
Hall & Oates,
and now this Foreigner song,
I'm restless to find poetry
in a more modern surrounding.

If it was 10:30 p.m.
and the place was lit
only by the neon OPEN sign,
I could endure
the radio station's poor choices.
And I would be happy
to show you
what love is.

The Couple

She leaned in,
her face chiseled
in love for him,
nodding at his sentences,
her eyebrows two swells
of a heart,
her whitened hair slicked back
in a ponytail
so her face is open to him.
When they sat down
at the café table,
they bent into a long kiss,
the Christmas tree
blinking behind them.
When she got up
to go to the counter,
she walked around to his side
and kissed him on the forehead,
his head tilted back
so he could feel it more.
And then I looked back
at my own world,
the pen in my hand,
and my love smiling at me
from across the table,
seeing it, too.

New Heaven

I stare at the candle flame
like it's a new heaven
and the crimson shadows
of perfume bottles
are really the face of the
Virgin Mary dancing,
singing
I was never a virgin
and
I prefer whiskey to wine
and
I've stayed up late so many nights
with new men
and
I am tired of moving in long skirts
and
I want to let my hair loose
and

God,
it is so hot
in here

the flames,
so close.

My Favorite Otis Redding Song

When the song came on
the radio, Thursday morning blues,
I thought of that night
driving back from the poetry
reading and you were in
the backseat with your girl
and everyone but me was drunk.
It was suggested we stop
at the dive bar
off the country highway
as a joke that became a dare.

When we walked in,
it was like in those movies
when the new stranger in town
swaggers into the local bar
in his denim jacket
and orders a beer
by just saying
"I'll have a beer" and
the bartender slides a beer
across the bar
and it's always the right one,
and everyone in the bar
immediately either hates
him or falls
in love with him.

That night I was the former,
at least to that woman
who scolded her man
for talking to me

....

about geography
while she sat at the end
of the bar
burning a hole through me
with her cigarette-lit eyes,
smoldering in junior high jealousy.

But we didn't give a shit
because me and your girl
made up a dance routine
to that Eurythmics song
and we kept ordering
rounds of Corona Light, all of us
in love with everything the night
shone down on us.

So when the song came on
the radio
I thought of all of that,

those small moments—
how they can stack up to
something big
in the heart's
memory—
and how that night
you played that song
on the jukebox

just for me

and thought I didn't notice.

....

This Kind of Quiet

It's midnight
on Friday and the weekend
is spread out like a smoothly
made bed with the covers
tucked up, waiting for me
to slide in, and that's exactly
what I'll do.
While you're out in the night
where quiet is the steady
stream of drunken voices
and cheap beers
slamming down on counters,
and you knock a few back
yourself, comforted
by this kind of quiet,
fighting to fill your head
with the right answers,
dousing your heart
with another shot of fuel
and one more song
to keep it running,

each of us enjoying
the kind of quiet
we deserve.

Everyday Wonders

My life gleams
with dusty roads
and the instrument of crickets,
with the moon as streetlamp
through my second-story window
and the smell of coffee when I rise
late on Saturdays.
Just today
I thought about all that,
driving my mud-splattered
10-year-old car
to the park
with the only child
I will ever have,
and I think I was wearing sweats
and walking shoes
and I'm pretty sure
my hair was stuck
in a ponytail
to hide its inadequacies,
and no one
gave me a second look
at the gas station.

But I think he will love me
no matter what.
And so will my little girl
made of butterfly and honey,
the three of us filling up our earth
with our own blooms
of extraordinary
everyday
wonders.

Riding Home

The hum
settles beneath me
into swaying valleys
and hills,
lullabying me into
a treasured cove.
My eyes catch
the next light beam, thin,
through my window,
its erratic pattern
as comforting
as the moon.
The sound of my parents
talking in the front seat,

the gods of my movable world.

I curl up tight
in the flat back
of the station wagon
and hug the night.
Everything
I love is here:
my parents' chatter,
my very own framed sky,
sleep like I'll never know again—
the warm ease of it all.
Rocked in the arms of the road
and then the cocoon
of my father's fleece coat
as I'm carried
home.

....

Unfaithful in a Good Way

for my husband

Even though your tulips
bloom in the glass vase,
and your love note
still sticks to the back
of the door,
I cheat on you
every night
in my dreams.

There,
I am who I never want to be.
I am brutal and careless,
torn between sneaking around
upstairs in dark rooms
in foreign hotels,
and going to you.

I awake in early hours,
breathless,
in our bed.
Thankful for the
soothing whisper
of the faithful
moon
and your breathing
in sleep.

My only crime:
I am addicted
to falling in love with you
again
and again.

....

Here I Am

Naked window
exposes starlight
for all of its worth.
Sheets rumpled at our feet
waiting for a breeze
through window's
open mouth.
Confused crickets
chirp to
car sounds,
the pages of his
book turn,
my wishes for the day
lain down
on the pillow,
the song from the radio
no longer
my body's music—
I am emptied
of all the seconds
that led to this one
when I will shed
my proper self,
and take
his hands.

....

The Chords of Our Desire

The moment
we can no longer
quiet the chords
of our desire,
we will clank
together—
my waist over
your brass tongue,
ringing with
long
resolution.

Julie Valin is a literary harlot. When she isn't writing poetry, reading two books at once, playing Scramble With Friends on her smart phone, or reading bedtime books to her little girl, Julie is a freelance copy editor, book designer, Poet in the Schools, and co-publisher and editor of Six Ft. Swells Press. She can switch between Pink Martini and Dinosaur Jr. faster than you can say *chimichanga*. You can find more information about her at *www.TheWordBoutique.net*.

Made in the USA
Middletown, DE
28 January 2022

59907854R00031